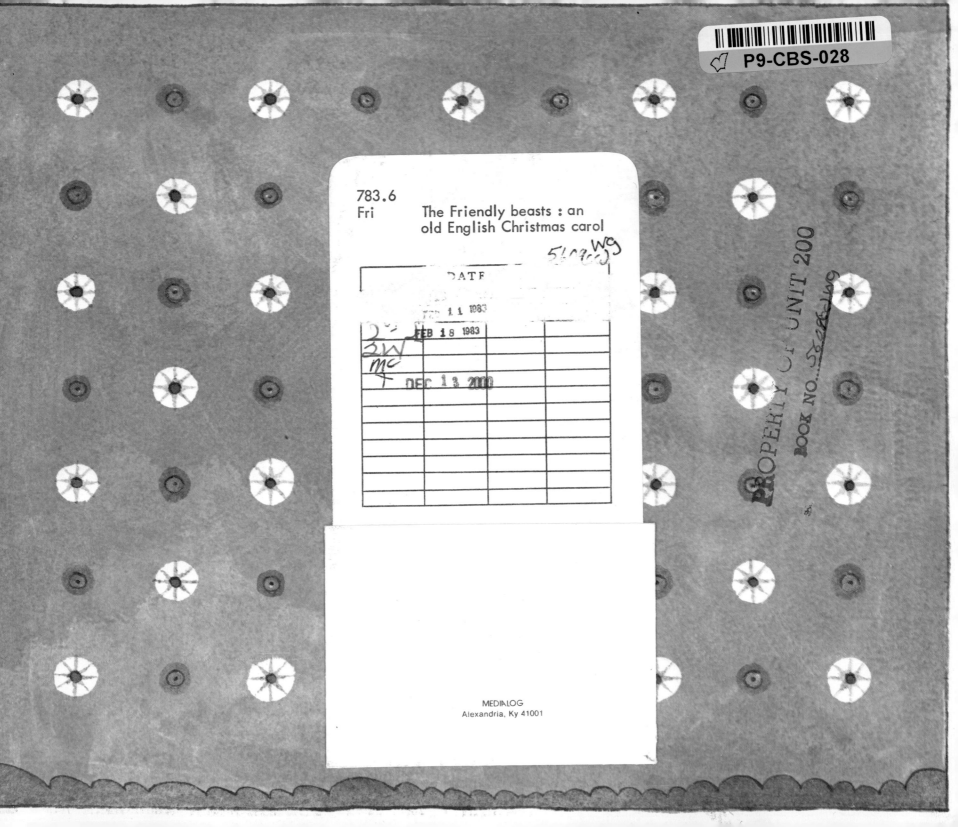

The Friendly Beasts

The Friendly Beasts

an old English Christmas Carol

Illustrations by
Tomie dePaola

G.P. Putnam's Sons · New York

Illustrations copyright © 1981 by Tomie de Paola.
All rights reserved. Published simultaneously in
Canada by General Publishing Co. Limited, Toronto.
Printed in the United States of America.
Library of Congress Cataloging in Publication Data
Main entry under title:
The Friendly beasts.
Summary: In this old English Christmas carol the
friendly stable beasts tell of the gifts they have given
to the newborn Jesus.
[1. Carols. English. 2. Christmas music.
3. Folk songs. English] I. De Paola. Tomie.
PZ8.3.F9118 783.6'5 80-15391
ISBN 0-399-20739-2
ISBN 0-399-20777-5 pbk.
First Peppercorn paperback edition published in 1981.
Second impression

for Wolfgang and Hanni

Jesus our brother, strong and good,
Was humbly born in a stable rude;
And the friendly beasts around Him stood,
Jesus our brother, strong and good.

"I," said the donkey, shaggy and brown,
"I carried His mother up hill and down;
"I carried her safely to Bethlehem town,
"I," said the donkey, shaggy and brown.

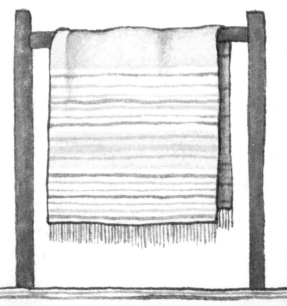

"I", said the cow, all white and red,
"I gave Him my manger for His bed;
"I gave Him my hay to pillow His head;
"I said the cow, all white and red.

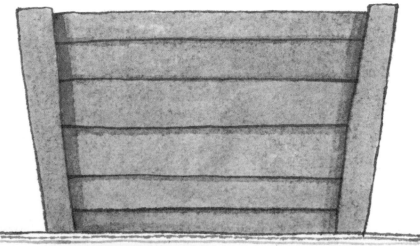

"I", said the sheep with curly horn,
"I gave Him my wool for His blanket warm.
"He wore my coat on Christmas morn,
"I", said the sheep with curly horn.

"I", said the dove from rafters high.
"I cooed Him to sleep so He would not cry,
"We cooed Him to sleep, my mate and I;
"I", said the dove from rafters high.

And every beast, by some good spell,
In the stable dark was glad to tell,
Of the gift he gave Emmanuel,
The gift he gave Emmanuel.

The Friendly Beasts

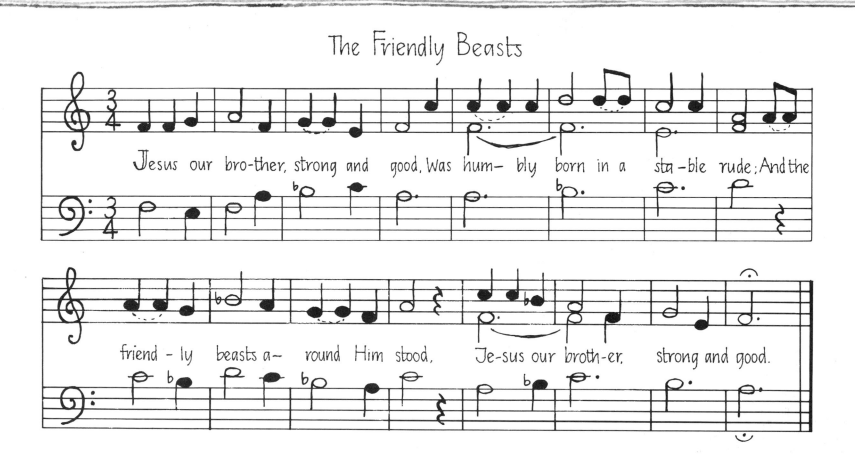

Jesus our bro-ther, strong and good, Was hum— bly born in a sta –ble rude; And the friend – ly beasts a— round Him stood, Je-sus our broth-er, strong and good.

"I", said the donkey, shaggy and brown,
"I carried His mother up hill and down;
"I carried her safely to Bethlehem town,
"I", said the donkey, shaggy and brown.

"I", said the cow, all white and red,
"I gave Him my manger for His bed;
"I gave Him my hay to pillow His head;
"I said the cow, all white and red.

"I", said the sheep with curly horn,
"I gave Him my wool for His blanket warm.
"He wore my coat on Christmas morn,
"I", said the sheep with curly horn.

"I", said the dove from rafters high.
"I cooed Him to sleep so He would not cry,
"We cooed Him to sleep, my mate and I;
"I", said the dove from rafters high.

And every beast, by some good spell,
In the stable dark was glad to tell,
Of the gift he gave Emmanuel,
The gift he gave Emmanuel.

The paintings for THE FRIENDLY BEASTS were done on 140 pound Fabriano handmade watercolor paper. The artist used transparent inks for the paintings, and handlettered the type. The printing was done by offset on 80 pound Mountie Matte, manufactured by Northwest Paper Co. and supplied by Alling & Cory. The separations were made by Capper Engraving. The book was printed by Rae Lithographers, and bound by Economy Bookbinders.

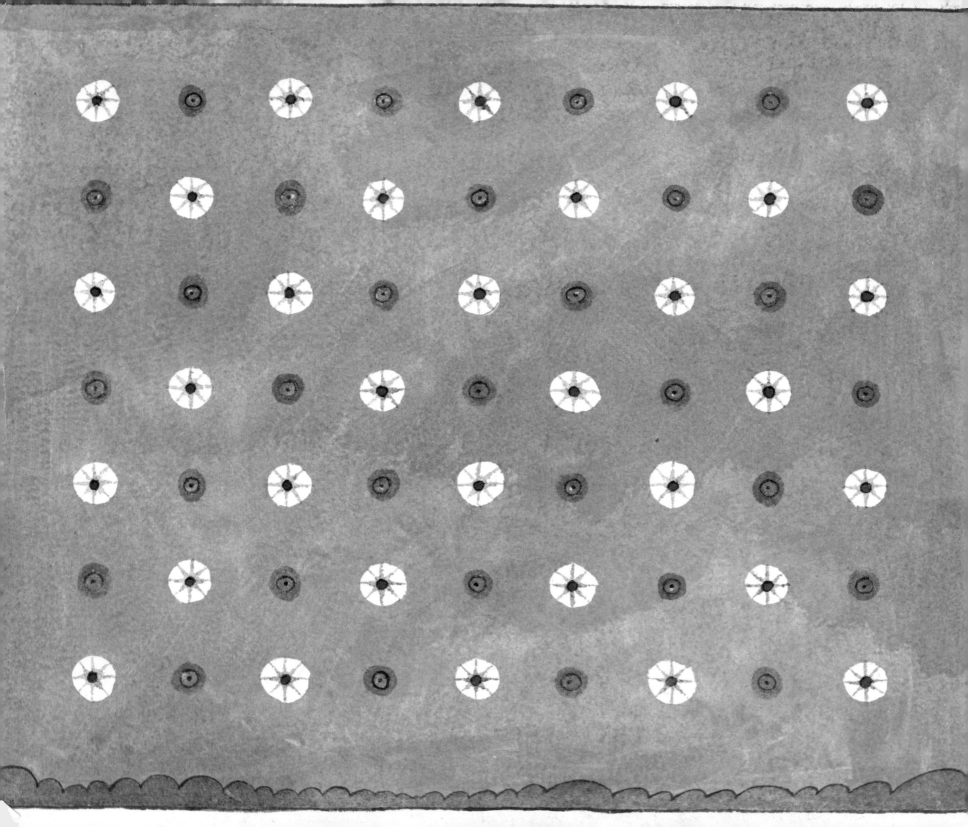